Culture Crossroads

Dealing with the pressures and demands on Pacific Islanders living in Aotearoa

Rubinstine Manukia

Copyright © 2021 Rubinstine Manukia
All rights reserved.

Edited by Sibley Schaumkell

The opinions expressed in this book are the author's own
and do not necessarily represent those of the
Methodist Church of New Zealand
– Te Haahi Weteriana O Aotearoa
or the publisher.

The author and publisher gratefully
acknowledge the financial support of the
Methodist Church of New Zealand

International print edition 2021
ISBN 978-1-98-857275-8

Philip Garside Publishing Ltd
PO Box 17160
Wellington 6147
New Zealand

books@pgpl.co.nz — www.pgpl.co.nz
eBook editions also available

Contents

Introduction 5
Preface 7
1 – The Pasifika Concept of Giving 9
    Challenging the Concept of Giving – A New Generation 9
    Balancing the Concept of Giving – Old vs New Generations 10
    The View of Polynesian Professionals 11
    The View of Clergy and Pacific Presbyters 12
    Misinale – Celebrates Tongan Financial Giving 16
    Public Perception of Giving 16

2 – Change Starts in the Home 18
    The Neuroscience of Learning Starts at Home 18
    Youth Today 19

3 – Christian Faith in the Workplace 21
    Christian Faith at Work 21
    The Art of Communication 22

4 – The intersection of Church and State 24
    United States Constitution vs New Zealand Law 24
    Pasifika Concerns About Recent Social Legislation 26
    Further Pasifika Concerns About the
    End Of Life Choice Act 2019 27

5 – Life beyond the Family 29
    Church as a village 29
    New Structures 29
    A legal framework in New Zealand 30

6 – Can we learn from a comparison with other systems
of Church? 32
    Tikanga Māori 33

7 – The direction of the Church for Pasifika peoples ... 35
    Pasifika faith lore 35
    Acculturation 36
    Further understanding 36
    Cultural Competence 37

    Diversity at Work 39
    Enablement through Community Led Development Principles
    (CLDP) 40
    Māori community development 41

8 – The current context 42
    Community development practice in Aotearoa today.................... 42
        Social Justice 42
        Individual and collective human rights 42
        Equity... 42
        Self-determination and empowerment 43
        Participation and democracy... 43
        Cooperation/collective action 43
        Sustainability (including, but not exclusively,
        environmental sustainability).. 43
    Bi-cultural community development practice in Aotearoa........... 43
    Enabling and Building Capacity 44

9 – Reflection – Lessons learned 46
    Learning from our situations 48
    Finding your own voice and pathway in life 49
    Epistemology of Pasifika People – Native Common Sense 49
    Hidden Meaning and Interpretation – Pasifika use of Sarcasm ... 49
    Unbroken – To know we belong 50
    Placemaking For Redemption – Making something better and
    more acceptable.. 51
    Learning by Doing and Empowerment 51

Conclusion 52

Appendix 53
  Sermon delivered by Rubinstine Manukia
  on Sunday 20 January 2019 at
  Pulela'a New Lynn Tongan Methodist Church 53

Endnotes 61

Index 63

Introduction

The idea for this book has emerged from 40 years of Methodism and my first-hand experience of growing up in a Christian family with Tongan values, culture, and traditions.

I grew up in a family where I witnessed the love of my parents for God, the Church and community. My father served as a Methodist Church steward for over 30 years. That love extended to the community and country we lived in, Aotearoa New Zealand, and our country of origin Tonga.

I begrudged that my parents sacrificed so much for the Church, which impacted on my adolescent years. It was the norm in my family to attend Church every Wednesday, Church cell group every Thursday, and youth activities every Friday. We cleaned the Church premises (including the toilets and hall) every Saturday. We attended Sunday school and the main service every Sunday. This was the cycle of my life growing up in a Christian household and I learned to accept it at an early age. I grew up believing that it was my culture and that I was bound by it. My siblings accepted the family routine without question. I on the other hand was less tolerant and more vocal in expressing my views and opinions. This sometimes landed me in hot water for challenging the family routine. I was a curious child with many questions about why, why, and why?

I questioned why we had to always attend Church; why we spent so much time at Church; why we had to tidy up after Church (when it seemed no one else had to clean up); why we had to participate in *Fakame* (the White Sunday celebration for children); why we had to always give money to the Church for *Misinale* (annual tithing). I had so many unanswered questions as a young child and don't recall ever receiving a satisfactory answer. Except that I was taught "everything we owned and earned belonged to God" and that if we contributed whole heartedly, we would reap what we had sown. This teaching was hard for a curious young girl to fathom in the 1980s and 1990s.

Today, while I can better understand the values and principles instilled by my parents about faith, family, and community, I don't adhere to them as rigidly with my own family as they did. Attending every church service is not always practical and missing a service is not a big issue. Our church now has a house steward who does the cleaning, whereas my father played the role of house steward and had us do the cleaning, even though he was head steward. I try my best to explain the meaning of White Sunday to my children and encourage them to participate in *Fakame*, but I don't force them to take part if they don't want to. However, I agree with annual tithing and contribute 10 percent of what I earn in tithings for *Misinale* each year.

Preface

Many Pasifika people feel under pressure in their lives in Aotearoa. When you migrate to a new country it is difficult to adapt to the new culture. Assimilating to the dominant culture is challenging.

In response to the demands of a new country, new culture and new surrounding neighbours, many older Pasifika people and those raised in the islands, choose to run their Aotearoa churches, and take part in the life of their church in the same way they did in the islands. This brings them comfort and a feeling of security.

Young Pasifika people born or raised mainly in Aotearoa are caught between the expectations of their parents and wider family to adhere to island culture and traditions and wanting to live a more relaxed kiwi lifestyle.

Successful Pasifika sports people, and professionals in other fields, are expected to give money to their extended family in Aotearoa and in the islands. In some extreme cases this pressure has caused young pacific youth and sports people to suicide.

Younger Aotearoa Pasifika people need to learn to put the needs of their immediate family and children first and be disciplined in how they handle their finances.

In this book, I propose that Churches in Aotearoa should have the right under the law of the country to decide for themselves on theological and ethical issues.

Churches own law courts and regulations should be recognised in statutes, as well as in the developing case law precedents. In the case of the Methodist Church our court is Conference, and the laws are documented in the *Laws and Regulations of the Methodist Church of New Zealand – Te Haahi Weteriana O Aotearoa.*[1]

As a subset of this, Pasifika church members should have the right to adopt their own theological and ethical rules on key social issues such as cannabis use, assisted dying, same sex marriage and abortion.

Members of other faiths and cultures in Aotearoa should also have the right to decide for themselves on theological and ethical issues.

But, if this is taken to extremes, and handled badly, there could be serious clashes between secular statutes and regulations, and church or faith-based courts and justice systems.

Muslim people for example, might call for the introduction of Sharia law to govern their communities in Aotearoa, which could limit the rights and freedoms that Muslim women have under New Zealand law.

There is ongoing political and social debate as to whether Māori should be entitled to run their own iwi based justice systems.

These issues feed into an argument that Aotearoa should have a written constitution that acknowledges the tenets of all faiths, religions, cultures and ethnicities.

1 – The Pasifika Concept of Giving

I grew up in a household believing that giving should be sacrificial. That serving God had everlasting effects and service was about being faithful. I experienced God always being there for my family. God provided the fundamental basic necessities in life, such as shelter, food, and clothing. I don't recall experiencing a time when I felt God had forsaken us. There were times when I wished that we had more in material abundance, but I was taught to aspire to make a difference and serve God, rather than aspire to make a fortune for myself. This resonates with me, and I live to make a difference and do things that really matter and have a lasting impact.

Challenging the Concept of Giving – A New Generation

My concept of giving changed when I reached adulthood and started my own family. Having children changed my priorities and outlook on life. Putting God first is my top priority and I do things differently from how I was raised. I make my children's personal, school, and educational needs a priority, including their extra-curricular activities. I am a dedicated sports Mum and an ardent sports fan. I support my children in their rugby, athletics, rowing, swimming, basketball, netball, gymnastics, and other activities.

I am a proud mother supportive of my family. I believe that spending quality time with your children and family is key for the growth and personal development of each individual for family unity. It is vital to have a personal relationship with our children, to gain their trust and confidence. To ensure that our children can turn to us when they face challenges, rather than turn away or to social media and the influences of the outside world. I count it a blessing to be able to attend my children's school activities. My parents were not always available for my siblings and I due to the demands of the Tongan church and their responsibilities as church stewards. I knew my parents cared but their priority was the church.

I don't believe there is only one way of balancing our commitments with the church and our families. No one size fits all. Intergenerational priorities have changed over the years. Now younger generations are putting more emphasis on what matters to them and their families before other commitments. I spoke to some Pasifika young people over

18-years-old. They were selected from a group of youth born in Aotearoa and overseas. Some of the participants were enrolled at universities, unemployed and looking for work.

I was interested to see what their priorities were and asked them what was important to them?

Tina from the University of Auckland said,

> "My priority is with my family and education. My education is my focus to make my parents proud."

Vili from Auckland University of Technology said,

> "My priority is with God, my family, sports and school. I have to work hard to provide a good living for me and my family."

Sam was unemployed and said,

> "My priority is to find a job. I dropped out of school without a qualification. My parents were disappointed in me, so I have to go and find work to support the family."

Alesi was unemployed and said,

> "My priority is to enrol in a trade course to upskill and increase my chances of getting a job. I left school young, without gaining a qualification and have to make ends meet."

Only one of the four people I spoke to mentioned God first in the mix. None of the four people mentioned the Church as a priority. If God and the Church were a priority, they were not acknowledged in the responses. The majority of the youth said that their families, their education, and jobs were important.

Balancing the Concept of Giving – Old vs New Generations

The Church was a priority for most traditional Pasifika Christian families from the early 1950s to the 1990s. Today, in the 21st century, priorities have changed among the younger generation and Aotearoa born Pasifika youth. Younger Pasifika parents have made their families a priority. These families have become more innovative, entrepreneurial, and enterprising.

The older Pasifika generation on the other hand are reluctant to relinquish and renounce the Pasifika way of life they were used to in their island villages. They favour holding on to the culture and traditions of the Pacific Islands.

The View of Polynesian Professionals

In an in-depth online article on *Stuff News* in 2015, Liam Napier explored the plight of Pacific Island professional sportsmen.[2]

Polynesian athletes faced pressures and demands to give back to their families because of the high expectation upon them to provide for their families.

For example, Manu Vatuvei and Jerome Kaino are among high profile sports stars who have given back to look after their families.

Giving back can be a burden and a blessing in Pacific Island culture. *Fa'alavelave* is the Samoan tradition where family and friends contribute money or gifts for major events – pulling together to support close family. *Tokoni'i* or *Fetokoni'aki* is the Tongan tradition for helping each other, assisting, and supporting one another.

This is not just a Samoan and Tongan concept. Many of the Pacific Island people adopt this communal culture based on everyone chipping in.

At the basic level it means that when you have good fortune, you look after others. When you hit hard times, the village or community is there to meet your needs.

There is huge pressure on Pasifika children and young people to provide for their families, especially when they have lucrative jobs where they earn a lot of money.

I spoke to Pasifika professionals from different vocations to get their views and insights on family demands and pressures living in Aotearoa, and these were some of their responses:

Tom a family doctor said,

> "I'm in a privileged position to help my parents and family with their basic needs, but I don't support them giving money to the Church or extended family in the islands."

Ana a criminal lawyer said,

> "I supports my parents, younger siblings and family financially, but I don't attend Church. I do not support giving money to the Church because the money I give my parents is for their mortgage, food and health."

Pita a hairdresser said,

> "I support my parents and brothers. I don't make much, but the little I make I give to my parents to spend wisely on my siblings. I'm not aware if they spend it on the Church, but if they did it wouldn't be much and would not be fair for my brothers."

Saane a nurse said,

> "I support my Church and parents financially. I give annually in tithings to my Church and help my parents with their Church tithings. I'm happy to provide this support because I'm the eldest of three sisters and my parents rely on me for help."

The majority of people I spoke to said they helped their families and only one of the four supported the Church through tithings. Two were born in the islands and two were born in Aotearoa.

The View of Clergy and Pacific Presbyters

Reverend Goll Fan Manukia of the Lotofale'ia Mangere Tongan Methodist Church, said,

> "We can say it's the culture but it's all about love and caring for the family."

He further said that,

> "Young Pacific Island people are brought up through the Christian values to love and care for each other and give to everyone."

For the majority of professional Pacific Island athletes around the world, giving back is a way of life. They play to secure their futures and those of their extended families.

This can place immense pressure on young athletes. Tensions build when the giving all seems one way, and when the hand is outstretched too often and too early.

At the absolute tragic worst, these situations have led to suicides. Pasifika athletes are among the six Australian National Rugby League-contracted players – all under the age of 21 – who have died in recent years.

Mosese Fotuaika (RIP) was one who found the pressure too much and took his own life. After toiling away in reserve grade, he was given his shot at the top-level Wests Tigers NRL team. But during pre-season training, the 20-year-old tore a pectoral muscle. His body was found by his pregnant girlfriend.

For many young athletes, the demands of sport are tougher mentally than physically. Living away from home in a year-by-year existence is difficult enough without being weighed down by providing for families and extended families.

Rev Goll Fan Manukia, further said that,

> "The custom of giving back to the community is an important part of Pasifika culture."

Although this is true, the question of where we should draw the line is what this book is about. How can we manage culture, customs, and traditions without comprising health, safety, well-being, and life?

Rev Vaitu'ulala Ngahe of the Manurewa Methodist Parish sees giving differently in a new way of thinking.

> "When you compare giving in Tonga – there was not much money. People worked hard on their plantations to grow crops and gave their harvests instead of money in offerings. In Aotearoa, it is totally different. In the ministry for the family (*fāmili*), if we don't feed our families first, then how can we feed others?
>
> There has to be a reserve for the families to put a bit aside for a rainy day and explore other available avenues and help from the outside. The Church should also have a reserve as a plan for a rainy day to support people who contribute annually. We must take care of them because if we don't, how will they contribute next year?"

Vaitu'ulala believes in tapping into the skills of people from within the Parish and wider community. He said,

> "The same principle of giving applies to the *Misinale* (Tongan annual tithing). It is not a competition and leaders should know which families can and cannot afford to give a large tithe, so that we don't lose those people because of the competition."

In many instances where Pacific Islanders earn much more than their peers or counterparts, they are expected to help their families, extended families, villages, and communities.

Often, as soon as a young family member obtains any professional sporting contract, or a modest tier-two international salary, there are immediate expectations that those funds will filter into the village and family.

The financial burden on many Pacific Islanders only heightens anxiety, weighing heavily on the shoulders of young families, many of whom are too shy to voice their concerns and feelings. Many struggle to adjust to all-consuming professional environments and the demands of the Church, family, village, and community.

With traditionally large families to provide for and parents retiring young, (sometimes as soon as parents feel their child has made it), the expectations and demands become enormous.

Some of Aotearoa's highest-profile sports people, the likes of retired Warriors and Kiwis star Manu Vatuvei, former All Blacks flanker Jerome Kaino and heavyweight boxer Joseph Parker, accept these traditional responsibilities.

Pacific Island cultures are inherently competitive. This stretches into the Church, which plays a large role in traditional life.

In some Churches, donations are regularly read out during service, and if a family of a sports player isn't giving generously, questions are asked, and shame is heaped on them. However, some of the Churches have scrapped this method of giving, which then puts less pressure on its members.

Some of the church leaders, presbyters and ministers I spoke to said,

> "Church tithings and donations are an integral part of church life. That it was necessary for the survival and sustainability of the functions and operations of the church, regardless of which church you belonged to."

Tana Umaga, the first New Zealander of Samoan heritage to captain the All Blacks, conveyed his frustrations with traditional customs in his 2008 biography *Up Close*.[3]

Umaga ventured back to Samoa for the first time since he was four with the Aotearoa A team in 1998. After the match he visited his father's family, whom he had never met. He had saved up some money and, after spending the morning with them, handed it over.

When Umaga returned home his father told him his uncle was "very disappointed" with the amount of money given – because he wanted a new truck. Umaga told his father to give his brother a message: that if he wanted a new truck, he and his kids should earn the money themselves.

When Umaga became a professional rugby player, he told his parents they'd never have anything to worry about but that his own kids weren't going to miss out because money had been passed on to the Church or someone else.

This Polynesian concept of giving back extends to many other careers, people such as lawyers, doctors, and school teachers, and even to factory workers. But because of their public profile and perceived salaries, those in the sporting sphere and other high profile professions are relied on more.

The average non-Pasifika person does not have the same degree of pressure, expectations and demands on them, especially financially.

As the aftermath of Jonah Lomu's death shows, super-stardom does not always guarantee you sustainable financial security. It is difficult to secure your own future while paying for others.

Rev Goll Fan Manukia commented that,

> "Individually we are all different. It's about how they are brought up and the values that are installed in them. That's what makes them want to give or not. If their parents are asking all the time, that would be a burden. If they are doing it out of their own free will, they count it as a blessing."

Although there is truth in that, it will not be accepted by everyone.

A lot of these athletes, and Pacific Island professionals, want to reduce the pressure at home, and their number one priority is to look after their families.

For the most part exchanges are authentic and done out of love. But there needs to be a better understanding of the pressures and demands that expectations from the wider family can cause, particularly in the early stages of a professional career, when wages aren't what they seem or when the money runs out.

Misinale – Celebrates Tongan Financial Giving

Misinale is the Tongan word for the traditional, annual celebration of donations of money to the church practiced today by Tongan churches all over the world. This Christian giving system in Tonga was introduced by early missionaries as a Biblical view of generous giving and was highly encouraged as God's standard of giving. I grew up with this Tongan financial donation system in my local church Pulela'a New Lynn Tongan Methodist Church.

I grew up thinking that it was the norm, but I questioned it? I don't recall exactly why I questioned it, but I had a feeling that something about it wasn't right? When I reached the age of 25, I began to deeply think seriously about why I questioned the *Misinale* system.

I believed there was nothing wrong with the *Misinale* system, but that people should contribute only what they can actually afford, without borrowing. Quick loan schemes and loan sharks should be avoided. People need to be frugal and more vigilant about their circumstances and financial means. The Church has a role to play in ensuring that its messages, notices, and communications aren't perceived by congregation members as directives, orders, demands or ultimatums.

Public Perception of Giving

The views of the general public are divided: some are sympathetic towards the professional players and blame the Church for taking their money; while others support a culture of giving, sharing, and caring for your family. There needs to be a balance between the two. This brings me to examine the role of churches and what they can do to help struggling families cope with the pressures and demands on them.

The Role of the Church to support Families

I believe the Church's role is to provide pastoral care and support. The Church has a pastoral responsibility to provide care and support for its congregants and parishioners, including those that seek help.

The greatest command in the bible revolves around love and care.

> "Teacher, which is the greatest commandment in the Law?"
>
> Jesus replied: 'Love the Lord your God with all your heart and with all your soul and with all your mind.' This is the first and greatest commandment. And the second is like

it: 'Love your neighbour as yourself.' All the Law and the Prophets hang on these two commandments."

Matthew 22:36-40 New International Version (NIV)

However, the role of the Church differs among different age groups, cultures, denominations, and ethnicities.

I spoke with Sione from the Catholic Church on the role of the Church, and he perceived the role of the Church to be,

> "to help the people in need with food, shelter and water, the basic fundamental needs of people in Aotearoa."

Lina from the Anglican Church noted the role of the Church to be,

> "a spiritual one to assist with the spiritual well-being of its members and followers."

Taane from the Presbyterian Church sees the role of the Church to,

> "provide fellowship, to worship in faith and prayer."

Lita from the Baptist Church sees the role of the Church to be.

> "a caring one, filled with love for its fellow citizens and members."

Mele from the United Tongan Church said the Church's role is to,

> "help others in need, especially with their *kaveingas, putus, mali, fai'ahos*" (family funerals, weddings, and birthdays, etc.).

2 – Change Starts in the Home

I firmly believe that instruction, guidance and education, about good values, habits, and life choices, should begin in the home from an early age. Supporting learning at home is vital for a child's preparation and development before school starts. A parent's priority should be their children, their well-being, and development. Parents need to do all they can within their means to create a safe and happy learning environment at home.

John Wesley's advice remains relevant today:

> "Do all the good you can, in all the ways you can, to all the souls you can, in every place you can, at all the times you can, with all the zeal you can, as long as ever you can."

Creating good habits at home and demonstrating basic fundamental values, such as gratefulness, thankfulness, appreciation, respect, and caring for others, are qualities that should be instilled at home in a child's early life. Learning these basics, will improve a child's choices later in life. Children are better informed and aware of what's good for them.

Early learning should never be a burden on parents to provide the basic fundamentals at home. Learning does not need to involve a lot of material possessions. Learning can be made fun and affordable. The Ministry of Education in Aotearoa provides ideas for playing, talking, reading, drawing, and counting basics to support learning at home on their website.[4]

Resources on the Ministry of Education in Aotearoa's website,[5] show a direct link between health, well-being, and student achievement. Furthermore, increased physical activity in schools and their communities has significantly improved overall health and well-being.

The Neuroscience of Learning Starts at Home

I had the privilege to hear world renowned psychiatrist, neuroscientist, and best-selling author of *The Dolphin Parent: A Guide to Raising Healthy, Happy and Self-Motivated Kids*, Dr Shimi Kang, share her expertise. Dr Kang explained how we are living in the most rapidly changing, ultra-competitive, globally diverse, and socially connected era humans have ever known. Drawing on science and unforgettable stories,

Dr Kang illuminates the latest research-based methods for developing the new future-ready skills that will be needed to succeed.

I agree with her idea, that learning new future-ready skills for success begins now and starts in the home. We can learn so much from our children in a reciprocal and interactive relationship. I believe in a give and take relationship where there is open communication and dialogue between parents and children. This is particularly, important in Pasifika families where open communication is not always supported and encouraged. Pasifika children are taught in Tongan culture to obey their parents and people in authority (including faith leaders), to follow instructions and not to question, refute or critique instructions, teachings, or doctrines.

Dr Kang points out that as 21st century parents, we may feel that the skills our children need to succeed today are vastly different from when we were young children. I believe this is true. My parents, for example, lived in a different era, under different circumstances. I contend that the balance of culture and tradition versus the life skills required to succeed in this century is changing. I believe that there needs to be a balance, with different priorities based on each family's circumstances.

A culturally adept person learns both sets of rules and knows when to switch between them to survive. Most of the younger generation adopt this view, whereas the older generation are loyal to their culture and traditions cloned from their island villages. In the end, it is a balancing act of what works for each individual family.

The old Chinese proverb is true today and tomorrow – "Do not confine your children to your own learning, for they were born in another time."

Youth Today

Young people today want to connect to their friends and the world using social media and aspire to own the technology they need to make this possible. There are so many social media platforms available for children and youth that parents are finding it difficult to keep up with their children's demands for iPhones, smart watches, iPads, and computers.

Many schools also require students to use laptops and education software, such as Chromebook laptops and Google Classroom. Children can become disconnected from their parents and the rest of their families, who do not have access to this type of technology. Some children find themselves teaching their parents how to use it. Children are accustomed to this new era, while older generations are finding it hard to cope and keep up with changes to their culture arising from this new technology.

We saw this happening during the initial COVID-19 Level 4 Lockdown of March and April 2020, when we could not meet in person, but needed to communicate using telephone, email and online computer platforms like Zoom, Google Hangouts, Microsoft Teams and Skype, and social media such as Facebook, Instagram, Twitter and Tik Tok.

Young people need to balance the pressure and demands of living in Aotearoa, and navigate through a world of fast-paced, ever-changing technology.

3 – Christian Faith in the Workplace

Christian Faith at Work

I've been interested in the Integration Profile and God at Work research being conducted by Princeton University in the United States.[6]

The purpose of the study was to examine the Impact of the Intersection of Church Law and Secular Law in the Workplace. It looked at whether Church law adds extra pressures in the workplace for those who are bound by their Church's rules. Did those people bound by Church law react differently in the workplace, in comparison to those people bound by "God only at work," without also being members of a church or faith-based organisation? I was interested to learn whether people reacted differently if they are members of a Church, to the pressures and demands of that Church, (in a similar way to Pasifika traditions and faith lore), compared to the reactions of those that have no expectations on them from being part of a Church, except for a more generalised conviction and faith in God.

This research documents personal and collective efforts to integrate faith into workplaces; a social movement that includes and extends beyond personal ethics. The development of The Integration Profile (TIP) Faith and Work Integration Scale, which is designed to measure the multidimensional nature of faith expressions within workplace settings, measures the manifestations of faith, religion, and spirituality at the individual level.

The study is relevant for connecting religion and work in the secular sense to identify patterns and influences of work faith integration.

Religiosity can significantly impact human behaviour, yet little is known about how religious belief and practice integrate with work. The study surveyed Christian workers in the United States and found that work-faith integration was positively associated with organisational size. Denominational groups varied in their degree of integration but displayed similar patterns across dimensions of integration. Work-faith integration was manifest most strongly in integration related to the self, and somewhat less so in areas related to others and in transcendent aspects of work.[7] Respondents attributed spiritual disciplines and workplace mentors as salient influences of work-faith integration. The finding is relevant in relation to this book because the choices often exercised by Pasifika people while they are at work in the world are not only related to the self, but an aggregate of the person's faith, family relationships and cultural values. A person's choices are often influenced by the whole whanau, kainga or village. There is no one size fits all.

A person's commitment to giving and providing for others should arise from personal freedom and individual choice. We have seen earlier, that, in Pasifika culture, a high earner will often feel obliged to provide for their family and Church out of fear of being labelled unacceptable if they don't. However, we have also seen in Umaga's situation, that he was not afraid to exercise his individual level of freedom of choice. This is a helpful example, which encourages other Pacific Islanders, feeling pressured by their own family and Church expectations, to exercise their own level of individual freedom. Pacific Islanders need to get better at knowing when to say 'no' and giving only within their means.

The Art of Communication

Expressing one's faith should come from the heart. If Pacific Islanders, such as professional athletes, wish to provide for their parents and give back to the Church or community, it should come from the heart without force, duress, or obligation. The true essence of giving is to give willingly without anyone or anything putting pressure on you. In the same way, religious liberty is a gift from God, and is not dependent on toleration by the government. God is seen as a 'liberating deity' in Scripture who loves his people and cares about that relationship enough to create people free to say 'no.' Pacific Islanders should feel free to say 'no' when the pressures and demands on them become unbearable or burdensome on their families, marriages, and relationships.

Families should not feel pressured or be pushed into debt or bankruptcy to financially accommodate Church needs. Families should not have to mortgage their homes or borrow quick money from loan sharks to donate to the Church. Nor should anyone turn to crime to fund donations. Pasifika ministers should not be forceful in their rhetoric when asking for donations. Instead, Pasifika families need to be empowered to understand that they have a choice.

Most of these concerns arise in Pacific Island-based churches, who have established branches in Aotearoa, and use peer pressure to squeeze money out of followers.

Unlike mainline churches, such as the Presbyterian, Anglican, Catholic and Mormon churches, these churches do not have the financial and administrative backing of large national organisations to help fund their building projects. So they rely on donations from their members.

While some churches continue to exploit their members today, this must not become a model for Pacific Island churches in general.

4 – The intersection of Church and State

United States Constitution vs New Zealand Law

The freedom gifted by God is protected by political and constitutional institutions. The framers of the United States Constitution had a vision for national government that differed greatly from the example provided by the Puritans, who came to New England in search of religious freedom.

Aotearoa does not have a constitution like the United States, but it protects religious freedom under the Universal Declaration of Human Rights, the New Zealand Human Rights Act, and the New Zealand Bill of Rights Act. In addition, Aotearoa has also ratified numerous international United Nations treaties.

The framers of the United States Constitution created a document that only spoke of religion once – to ban religious tests for public office. The First Amendment to the Constitution, contains an "establishment of religion" clause, which means that neither a state nor the federal government can set up a church. Nor can they pass laws which aid one religion, aid all religions, or prefer one religion over another.

The First Amendment also forbids interference by the federal government or a state with the exercise of religion. These provisions must be taken seriously, and rigorously observed to protect religious freedoms and liberties.

Today in the United States, the relationship between church and state is an energetic one. Voices and viewpoints line up across the spectrum. Some would argue from history that there should be a 'wall of separation' between the two. While others maintain that co-existence is not only necessary and inevitable but can lead to positive results.

In real life, church and state do operate in similar spheres which gives rise to both conflicts and opportunities for cooperation.

The intersection of Church and State in Aotearoa has crossroads and roadblocks similar to those in the United States. The New Zealand parliament has passed legislation that impacts on theological beliefs, and religious dogma, as well as the culture and traditions of diverse communities. Where the two meet, there are cooperative ideals at work, as well as conflicts. This is similar to the intersection of early Pacific

Island migrant worshippers with New Zealand-raised Pacific Island worshippers. There have been clashes and struggles to find commonality in Aotearoa.

In the Pacific, families typically have long-standing connections with particular denominations and exert pressure on members to remain within them. In Aotearoa people are free to leave and join other denominations. However, people in Aotearoa are not just swapping denominations but leaving Church altogether. Nonetheless, Pacific Church communities are likely to remain a central feature of Pasifika enclaves in Aotearoa, and they will continue to adapt to the growing influence of Aotearoa-raised members.

The current high level of participation in Pasifika church communities may decline, as patterns of religious commitment for New Zealand-raised Pacific Islanders come to resemble those of the general population.

Pasifika athletes and sports stars face the same dilemma when they are torn between two worlds: that of their parent's generation and their own generation. Often, Pacific Islanders will abide by the obligations of their culture and tradition to please their parents, even when it is not what they would personally prefer to do. I believe, this is due in part to cultural and traditional expectations, and the need to show obedience and respect for your elders, i.e. your parents' *matu'a*, that demonstrates feelings of love and compassion for them. The choice to abide by one's culture and tradition is easy for many Pacific Islanders because they love and adore their parents, families, and extended families. This can also be demonstrated through service within their communities, which demonstrates leadership and mana in character.

Sir Michael Jones has expressed the meanings of giving in these terms. "To whom much is given much is expected." "The road to true leadership is through service." "…unless you know how to serve your people, you are not recognised as a leader." "Yes, it's a burden, but it's a burden of leadership." "It comes with you being a chief or matai in your family. Because of that, you are accorded a lot of benefits. You're looked up to and have the mana."

These obligations and responsibilities must be fulfilled because of your rank in the Church, village, community, or family.

Pasifika Concerns About Recent Social Legislation

There is a separation between Church and State, and the New Zealand Government has in recent years passed legislation that has rattled many church member's theological beliefs. For example, the Marriage (Definition of Marriage) Amendment Act 2013, the Shop Trading Hours Amendment Act 2016, End of Life Choice Act 2019, and the New Zealand Abortion Legislation Act 2020.

The reasons Pasifika people object to such legislation are varied:

- **The Marriage (Definition of Marriage) Amendment Act 2013** contradicts the word of God. In scripture the Bible says that marriage is between a man and a woman. The Bible defines marriage as a Covenant. The marriage ceremony, therefore, is meant to be a public demonstration of a couple's commitment to a covenant relationship. This demonstrates that both husband and wife see marriage as more than just a physical and emotional union, but also as a moral and legal commitment. The Bible defines Marriage as a Covenant. God sketched the original plan for marriage in Genesis 2:24 when one man (Adam) and one woman (Eve) united together to become one flesh. Therefore, a man shall leave his father and his mother and hold fast to his wife, and they shall become one flesh (Genesis 2:24).

- **The Shop Trading Hours Amendment Act 2016** contradicts the word of God. God created the world in six days, and on the seventh day, God rested (Genesis 1:1-2:2). This seventh day is the Sabbath day. When God gave Moses the Ten Commandments, one of His commandments was to "remember the Sabbath day, to keep it holy" (Exodus 20:8). The word Sabbath comes from a Hebrew word that means "to rest from labour." The word 'holy' means something that is sacred or dedicated to God. God wants us to make Sunday, the Sabbath day, feel different from the other days of the week by resting from our normal daily routine and dedicating our thoughts and time to God.

- **The New Zealand Abortion Legislation Act 2020** contradicts the word of God. The Bible describes the unborn child as a valuable life. King David illustrates this in Psalm 139. "For you created my inmost being; You knit me together in my mother's womb, I praise You because I am fearfully and wonderfully made; Your works are wonderful; I know that full well. My frame was not hidden from You when I was made in the secret place, when I was woven together in the depths of the earth." In addition, the sixth commandment states, "You shall not murder" (Exodus 20:13).

- **The End of Life Choice Act 2019** contradicts the word of God. For Christians, human life is sacred and is a gift from God which is to be respected and protected. This teaching is called the sanctity of life. The Bible teaches that human beings are created in the image of God. It also teaches that murder is forbidden. Life is a gift from God. Adam became a living being by the breath of God (Genesis 2:7), and if God were to withdraw his breath from humans, they would perish (Job 34:14-15). Since life belongs to God, humans do not have absolute autonomy over their own life but are stewards of the life given to them by God. The lives of all humans, both their own and others, are to be cherished and guarded. The value of human life is intrinsic, for it derives from God, who made human beings in his own image (Genesis 1:26-27). Consequently, the person who takes the life of another will be held accountable and punishable by God through his human representatives (Genesis 9:5-6; Romans 13:1-7).

Further Pasifika Concerns About the End Of Life Choice Act 2019

People of Pacific Island descent are concerned with the difficult ethical and cultural issues the Act will cause. They are concerned about a person's mental capacity to understand the nature and consequences of their end of life care options. For Pacific peoples there is no explanation or proper diagnosis for depression which is part of western *palangi* terminology. A mental health specialist will not be able to identify when the patient determines what 'unbearable suffering' means, which effectively legalises assisted suicide on demand for any condition, not just a terminal illness. This is a concern because depression is the most common reason people take this view of their condition. Depression is often poorly diagnosed and is potentially treatable.

Furthermore, the concern is that the Act causes social harm and is contradictory to the existing efforts of Pacific peoples to combat and reduce the current suicide rate among Pacific Islanders, which is at an all-time high in comparison to other OCED countries. How will this Act affect existing, successful programmes such as the: Toko Collaboration, Siaola and Famili Lelei initiatives?

Pacific people are also concerned about the provision that requires two doctors to agree with the request. Apparently in the US State of Oregon, the two-doctor safeguard has not worked because neither doctor may know the patient well enough to determine whether depression is present or if coercion is occurring. This is evident in diverse communities where language is a barrier and there are nuances of hidden meaning and interpretation, as for example in the Pasifika use of sarcasm (see Hidden Meaning and Interpretation – Pasifika use of Sarcasm in Chapter 9).

Rather than the approach taken by the Act, Pasifika people support the current palliative care system of organised health professional services and hospices for their precious elderly and the love and care of family support for individuals with terminal and other grievous illnesses. This is the system that Pasifika people are familiar with and can relate to in caring for their sick and terminally ill. It seems obvious that were a cheap, 'quick fix' alternative to be available instead, there would be much less incentive to research and provide high-quality palliative care.

There are other law-related problems with the Act. One very obvious one is the potential for coercion on the part of relatives or others who may well benefit from the death of the person concerned. Much of this pressure is subtle and cannot be detected by anyone outside the immediate family relationship, including doctors and social workers.

Another legal issue is the fact that the direct cause of death will not appear on death certificates, thereby falsifying them for those who die as a result of this legislation. This will also make it very difficult to collect accurate statistics as to the frequency of use of various lethal substances which are used to cause the death of the persons concerned.

Yet another issue is the role of the person who holds the Power of Attorney in relation to health care, where this exists. Is this the kind of person envisaged in section 9 (4) (c) of the Act who may sign the form in place of the affected person? With no certification required, this provision is ripe for abuse.

The Act is regarded as a danger to Pasifika communities. It is flawed and cannot be amended to make it safe.

5 – Life beyond the Family

The life of Pacific Islanders extends beyond the family unit, to the Church, village, community, extended family (whānau) and workplace.

For many Pasifika people, their religious beliefs are incorporated into a way of life, based on a culture of how Pasifika people normally do things.

Religion is mixed with culture and tradition and extends beyond the boundary of the Church for Pasifika people.

My observation is that palangi church members generally do not think of membership of the Church as extending as far into their personal lives as Pasifika people. Pasifika people generally view their Church in Aotearoa as fulfilling the same role as their village in the Islands.

Church as a village

Pacific Island community life and personal social identity are built around three closely integrated institutions for pacific people: family, church, and village. This structure has been recreated in Aotearoa with new or existing Church communities acting as surrogate villages. Those who had identified as members of a particular family, denomination, and village 'back home' can continue to do so. Within this structure the minister (*Faifekau*) or pastor (*Faifeau*) – the most powerful and respected figure in the Church community – is akin to a village chief. In many Pasifika Churches, the aim is to maintain the religious and cultural traditions of island life, rather than adapt to the Aotearoa New Zealand context.

Whether this is a good thing can be debated. For most Pacific people, the freedom of association and freedom of expression to worship in a culturally appropriate way in a foreign land, remains important. The concept of Church as a village remains the ideal approach for most Pacific churches.

New Structures

Many Pasifika people still want to follow a form of Christianity centred on Pacific Island traditions, culture, and language. So they clone, in Aotearoa, the village churches where they worshipped before arriving here. This Pasifika entitlement is protected under the rights and freedoms of the New Zealand Bill of Rights Act.

The First Amendment of the United States Constitution provides a "Freedom of Association" model that we can learn from. In a 2016 article, Laura Thompson writes:

> "The First Amendment is essentially a written guarantee that the government may not compel nor prohibit the exercise of religion in its state… Rather, that men and women would practice their religion of choice in their private lives, without the interference, guidance, support, or opposition of the government."[8]

At issue is whether this leads to the development of legal pluralism, where members of a religious faith, e.g. a Christian church, can claim that the laws and structures of their church take precedence for them over the nation's laws and statutes, which bind other citizens. While the United States government cannot declare an official religion, the inclusion into legislation of religious principles, Christian in particular, is not forbidden.

A legal framework in New Zealand

There should be an identifiable legal framework which recognises that religion, for Pasifika people, is central to their well-being, social and economic life. Pasifika people connect differently to Church and religion than other New Zealanders. The Church plays a vital role in the family and extended family life of Pasifika people. For Pasifika people, their faith in God defines their existence. For them, God is defined as the centre of all things on heaven and earth.

Pasifika people living in Aotearoa should be provided with a Church legal framework that enables them to adopt and retain the values and expressions of their culture and beliefs.

The membership of the Church in New Zealand is becoming more diverse. We need to move towards a multi-cultural 'legal framework of religion' for diverse cultures, including Pasifika people that will help shape the Church in the future. This remains a work in progress and more work is required to embrace a fully multi-cultural framework in response to the diversity of population and demographic trends in Aotearoa.

Our theology should respect and reflect the time and place we live in. Issues our new theology needs to embrace include:

- A commitment to a Bi-cultural journey that supports the Treaty of Waitangi.
- New expressions of power-sharing both structural and personal.
- Extension of social justice and positive interpersonal values throughout society, and
- Concern for the environment.

6 – Can we learn from a comparison with other systems of Church?

Churches in Aotearoa vary in the degree to which they have adopted, or preserved, the 'establishment,' or nexus of Church and State.

The Anglican Church in Aotearoa occupies a unique position in New Zealand society, in part because of the close links between that church and Māori. This in turn had its effect on the 'establishment' of the Church.

In Aotearoa, the Anglican Church has also often taken a leading role in promoting recognition of the Treaty of Waitangi, with its principle of partnership between Māori and Pakeha. Currently, the Treaty of Waitangi has socio political, but not legal force, as it is not a treaty recognised by international law. It therefore has effect only so far as legal recognition has been specifically accorded to it. At some time in the future, however, either the Courts or Parliament may have to give the Treaty legal recognition as part of a New Zealand constitution (a work-in-progress).

But already the Treaty of Waitangi, as a principle of the constitution, is now all but entrenched, if only because it is regarded by Māori generally as a sort of 'holy writ.'

In Aotearoa, churches have at least emphasised the Treaty of Waitangi, though not at the expense of losing their own apostolic and broad character. The Methodist Church of New Zealand – Te Haahi Weteriana O Aotearoa Bi-cultural Partnership Framework, gives recognition to people of the land, tangata whenua.

The legal, jurisdictional form of the Anglican Church is less apparent than it is in the Roman Catholic Church. But it is no less certain that the legal form of the Church of England has been important in its evolution.

In broad terms, the authority of the Church is not considered man-made law, but law derived from God, or divine law as revealed to human beings as is the canon law of the Church.

Yet much of the law governing the Church is to be found in secular statutes and court decisions, in accordance with the relationship between Church and State since the Reformation in England.

In comparison, the framework within which the Methodist Church of New Zealand – Te Haahi Weteriana O Aotearoa operates may be characterised by two factors. First, it is quasi-established in that it has been recognised by Court decisions (Mabon[9], Palu[10], et al.), and thus there are some legal links between Church and State. Secondly, it enjoys a privileged position under Mabon where the judge accepted the Church's submission that the civil courts are not equipped to answer theological questions and recognised that there is an ecclesiastical court to deal with such issues in the Methodist Church, i.e. its Conference.

The court decision in Mabon set a precedent by giving the Methodist Church legal recognition of its Conference and in Palu et. al., legal validity of Church property.

This tells us that the Church has considered the bi-cultural journey with Māori, and recognised diversity among the members of the Church. Pacific peoples are integral to the life of the Church in Aotearoa, and many have oversight of their own congregations and parishes, in their own ethnic languages, culture, and traditions. Thus, Pacific peoples have brought their villages, culture, and traditions from the Islands to the Church in Aotearoa.

Tikanga Māori

Prior to European settlement, the individual Māori tribes of Aotearoa had well-established governance arrangements, social structures, and systems of accepted norms and customs, generally referred to as Tikanga Māori.

Tikanga Māori included rules relating to trade and land rights, family relationships, protection of the environment, and conflict resolution.

The further development of a dual system of State secular law and Church law will require very clear guidelines from the outset, to eliminate any conceptual challenges to the legitimacy of a secular legal system (based on a state model if there is an alternative system claiming allegiance from within the same state). Similarly, whether State secular law will allow a separate Church law to control Church members generally or evolve a Pacific approach to deal with the pressures and strains on Pasifika people living in Aotearoa, or whether it will 'pose serious challenges to the State's ability to claim the allegiance of its citizens,' depends on the balance of powers and respect for one another's autonomy.

For example, Christians may argue that they owe a split form of allegiance in any event:

> Then Jesus said to them, "Give back to Caesar what is Caesar's and to God what is God's." *Mark 12:17 (NIV)*

New Zealand Methodists, among other faith denominations, may nonetheless argue that the State should, at a minimum, consult with the Church on all matters related and relevant to the Church before making laws and regulations. For instance, the voluntary euthanasia (The End of Life Choice Act), launched recently, by David Seymour was opposed on religious and cultural grounds by most Pasifika people. The threshold for determining what is regarded as relevant and related to the Church will be a high test.

The State should not be involved in deciding on theological questions on which only the Church can decide in its courts (see Mabon, Palu, et al.). There should ideally be a formal recognition that Church Law, in large measure, institutionalises this split allegiance. For example, Christians may argue that by amending legislation on marriage, the State was effectively usurping a matter which, so far as Christians are concerned, should lie solely within the realm of Church and canon law, for those who are bound by the Church and canon law.

I agree with Professor Norman Doe's proposal in his book *Christian Law: Contemporary Principles*[11] that all denominations of the Christian faith share common principles in spite of their doctrinal divisions; showing how dogmas may divide but laws may link Christians across traditions. The recognition of Church law, such as the Methodist Church of New Zealand's Laws and Regulations, will itself contribute to a theological understanding of a global Christian identity.

As an example, there should be State recognition of a separate Church law for Aotearoa Methodists to co-exist with New Zealand secular law concerning theological questions. This would be similar to various international sporting codes who are governed by their own International Arbitration and Court system. The Methodist Church of New Zealand should also have its own recognisable church law and ecclesiastical court (i.e. its Conference) to co-exist in harmony with New Zealand secular Law.

7 – The direction of the Church for Pasifika peoples

I am hopeful that the relationship between Church and State will evolve in a positive direction in future. We have seen how pivotal the Church and Christianity is to Pasifika people and their culture and traditions. So, too is a resurgence of interest in church law and a renewed interest in secular law relating to religion generally. Furthermore, we are living in a time when the world is not only defying God's laws, but trying to remove them completely from governments, schools, and public view.

I believe the culture and traditions of Pasifika people living in Aotearoa need to be part of the development of the law and be given clear recognition in the state legal system. It is certainly a time for a change and a response to the rapid growth of immigration, bringing refugees and diverse ethnicities into Aotearoa. Church law and alternative methods or models (in a national sense) will contribute to the future maturation of the New Zealand legal system.

The New Zealand legal and institutional systems should recognise Church law as part of the state's legal framework for identifying and resolving theological questions applicable to the Church. New Zealand Methodist Church law should be accepted within the New Zealand legal landscape and formally recognised as law to co-exist in harmony with New Zealand secular law.

The establishment of an effective body of national church law will acknowledge the identity and mission of the Christian Church and encourage ecumenical dialogue that will reach well beyond church law. This movement is essential in an uncertain time and to protect the vulnerability of countries under siege with the rise of war crimes, anarchy and terrorism undermining the autonomy and sanctity of religious dogma.

Pasifika faith lore

The Pasifika way of doing things challenges, exists alongside, and is subservient to the general secular law, but has a clear separate identity.

Pacific worldviews and paradigms support the legal debate between the

State and the concept of a separate legal system which acknowledges other existing systems and traditions of law, e.g. Pasifika faith lore.

Church law and Pasifika faith lore should be at the forefront of discussions about and awareness of a separate identity of law that can co-exist in harmony with the general secular law.

In the mental health arena, there is an increasing openness to developing services that are responsive to Pasifika people's cultural needs. The development of Pasifika models acknowledges the value of applying indigenous cultural values in contemporary settings.

Acculturation

Acculturation can be defined as the transfer of values and customs from one group to another. Tongan people dressing in western clothing is an example of acculturation, the modification of the culture of a group or individual as a result of contact with a different culture.

Understanding the patterns and trajectories of acculturation and its key impacts and determinants, is important for understanding cultural differences.

Further understanding

Sharing indigenous perspectives grounded in decolonisation, the struggle for social justice, cultural reclamation, and the development of indigenous knowledge, will help is to understand cultural differences. This offers an opportunity to view acculturation linked to cultural identity and reclaim and reconcile cultural differences.

Coming to live in Aotearoa – the land of milk and honey – is the dream of many Pasifika people. Expectations about Aotearoa were high, as Pasifika people dreamt of a better life here, spurred on by earlier Pasifika migrant family members, who retold their positive experiences of life in Aotearoa. Pasifika migrants came with the intention of improving the lives of their families and themselves. Starting with an understanding of Pasifika migrants isolated from their culture, the study of acculturation aims to explore and document how island-born Pasifika people acculturate to Aotearoa society.

Understanding individual stories and personal journeys highlights the acculturation processes that Pacific people go through to merge into Aotearoa society.

For example, my biography about my father's life, *Like a Dove*,[12] tells his story from the lens of a migrant to Aotearoa in search of better education opportunities for his family. We can learn from his journey and personal insights to better understand the acculturation process. He lived out his faith in God, love for family and passion for service.

Such insights, lead us to consider ways to alleviate negative experiences, and dispel prejudices, biases, and stereotypes about diverse communities.

The bigger picture brings us back to questioning the relevance and structure of a holistic lifestyle. For Pasifika people in Aotearoa, acculturation must be balanced so they benefit from the integration of Pasifika core values with the dominant culture.

Changing the acculturation conversation and indigenous cultural reclamation in Aotearoa

We must navigate not only acculturation in Aotearoa but also within our own indigenous kaupapa, and Pasifika customs, cultures, and traditions. Having to navigate two worlds is not a problem; instead, it reflects how many of us experience life in Aotearoa – we learn to navigate two spaces in order to be successful in today's world.

Reverends Vaitu'ulala Ngahe and 'Alipate Uhila, pastors in palangi congregations, still retain their pride and identity in being Tongan. 'Alipate is involved in Vahefonua Tonga o Aotearoa and the Tupou College Old Boys Association (Toloa) and Vaitu'ulala has strong ties to the Kingdom of Tonga and Tongan community in Aotearoa. We can also learn from insights that Reverend Siosifa Pole, who has ministered at Waterview, Wesley Roskill and Dunedin, offered in his 2020 book *Fisi'inaua 'i Vaha – A Tongan Migrant's Way*.[13] In a Pasifika paradigm and worldview, learning to navigate between two spaces is necessary for success and prosperity. Pasifika people who can operate in both their Pasifika context and that of mainstream New Zealand society will thrive in Aotearoa.

Cultural Competence

In Aotearoa there is a growing awareness that cultural competence is a key tool for making services more responsive to Pasifika people, Māori, and other ethnic groups.

For example, the health care system in Aotearoa has made cultural competence compulsory and a key requirement in their policies. District Health Boards and other regulatory bodies now have cultural competence polices. Pasifika health services have for many years implemented culturally competent Pasifika practice in their work places. Pasifika healthcare provider Fono Health and Social Services states that, "caring is our culture."

Increasing cultural competency is a shared responsibility that requires partnerships across a wide range of sectors – including health, social services, education, justice, and research – using systematic and sustainable approaches.

Cultural competence is important in the criminal justice system. In the prison setting, cultural competence enables prison officers to be more effective in supervising and managing inmates from diverse cultures and backgrounds.

Relationships are a powerful part of who we are. They can help make us feel that we belong and have something to contribute to this world. They can strengthen us. They give us a reason to affect change in our communities and to be changed ourselves. It's difficult to connect with people when we don't understand their background. So we need to interact respectfully and knowledgeably with all the people in our lives who exist outside our inner circle, and people whose culture and worldviews are different from our own.

People with diverse racial or ethnic backgrounds, refugees, migrants, and immigrants are all around us. That's the nature of the increasingly diverse and beautiful country in which we live.

Cultural competence is important because without it, our opportunity to build those cross-cultural relationships is impossible. Instead, we'll co-exist with people we don't understand, creating a higher risk of misunderstandings, hurt, biases, prejudices and stereotypes, that can be avoided.

People need to immerse themselves in learning about other cultures to grow in cultural competence. Diverse people bring new cultures, family histories, and different worldviews. The goal should be a willingness to share our own culture and learn about the culture of others.

Pasifika cultural competence should be considered integral to the definition of quality of care if we are to move towards quality outcomes. It could be included in accreditation tools, regulatory criteria, and national surveys. Quality indicators are required to identify, define, track, evaluate and improve culturally competent practices and services.

At present little is known about the feasibility and efficacy of Pasifika cultural competencies, i.e. do they work or not? For Pasifika people the issue is that cultural competencies lack rigorous evaluation, which means the most effective approaches for improving outcomes have not yet been identified. Increased research and study are recommended for achieving sound outcomes in the area of cultural competence.

Some specific areas that need to be researched are:

- How to define cultural competence?
- What are the elements of cultural competence?
- What are the barriers to cultural competence?
- How to measure cultural competence?
- What will improve cultural competence?
- How to apply cultural competence?
- Why cultural competence is relevant?

Diversity at Work

Diversity at Work is another platform that can be used to include structures, approaches, processes, and improved communication channels in our organisations, to help us address cultural differences, crossroads, nuances and diversity. Diversity is all around us; global economic trends, shifts in population structures, and diversity among cultures. The key to unlocking the social and economic benefits of diversity is through organisations having cultures of inclusion.

Organisations who have been on the diversity and inclusion journey now have many of the fundamentals around leadership and processes in place. In Aotearoa organisations like Global Women and Deloitte have partnered to discover how included New Zealanders feel at work and to understand what the drivers of inclusion are in seeking greater diversity and inclusion in order to enhance their performance, to better serve their customer base and to enable growth by tapping into a broader talent pool. Diversity without inclusion is typically short-lived.

Aotearoa is at a tipping point where bold moves around diversity will result in more rapid changes towards inclusiveness and acceptance. Embracing flexibility and diversity better serves the community. Conversely, the less diversity there is, the harder it is to change the culture. When their people feel included, organisations see improved business performance and better productivity. There are untapped benefits yet to be realised by Aotearoa organisations.

Enablement through Community Led Development Principles (CLDP)

Community Led Development Principles (CLDP) enablers are community development practitioners, who give people the skills, tools, and confidence to run sustainable, grassroots projects and organisations in their own community. Community enablers are hired and employed by different organisations across Aotearoa. For example, the not-for-profit and charitable sector, and the New Zealand Department of Internal Affairs.

Guided by the Principles, they work to develop vibrant, inspiring communities.

The framework for community development practice in Aotearoa was established in the 1935 to 1970s period, beginning with the establishment of the welfare system by the first Labour government. The Physical Welfare and Recreation Act 1937 (administered by the Internal Affairs Department) saw the establishment of the first community development programmes by government.[14]

In the 1970s community development units were set up in many local and regional authorities, as a result of a growing recognition of the need to find local solutions to local issues. The Local Government Act 1974 specified that local authorities should provide community development functions and these responsibilities were backed with central government funding.[15]

L. Chile (2006) suggests community development practice in New Zealand is best understood as three concurrent processes:

1. Community development programmes undertaken by the state (through government departments and authorities)

2. Processes of social change undertaken primarily through the collective action of individuals, groups, and organisations to give voice to marginalised groups and communities.

3. The forces of change within tangata whenua, Māori, working for tino rangatiratanga.[16]

Chile suggests that the dominance of the State as the provider sets the overall framework for community development practice through legislation that directs community development practice, provides funding, and devolves services to the community, voluntary and not-for-profit sector, that the State could not provide directly.

Māori community development

Māori community development has evolved out of hundreds of years of practice based on whānau, hapū and iwi groupings. Prior to European colonisation Māori were engaged in the development of their own communities, whānau, hapū and iwi. This development was a holistic process that did not divide body, mind, and soul and the physical from the non-physical, the individual from the group.[17]

Throughout the twentieth century, successive governments put in place legislative frameworks designed (in part) to assist Māori community development (e.g. the Māori Economic and Social Advancement Act 1945 and the Māori Welfare Act 1962). However, disparities in the well-being of Māori and non-Māori have continued. Chile suggests that while such initiatives provided great potential for Māori community development, they were not adequately funded.[18]

Government programmes to address inequalities in the wellbeing of the Māori population relative to the rest of the population, were also a feature of the early part of this century (e.g. Closing the Gaps and the Reducing Inequalities Strategy).[19] These initiatives resulted in a number of approaches to empowering Māori hapū and iwi to address their own priorities being trialled, including capacity building and community development type initiatives.

8 – The current context

Communities in Aotearoa are becoming increasingly diverse, with different communities facing different issues and cultural dilemmas. Issues arise from the impacts of acculturation, adaptation, and integration, heightened by social, economic, and cultural dilemmas and crossroads among migrant and ethnic communities.

Government and organisations in Aotearoa need to recognise that a 'one size fits all' approach is unlikely to be effective. They need to identify new ways of working with communities. An effective approach is to encourage community led practice and principles to guide community ownership and autonomy over local issues to be supported and funded by government.

The nature of community development work means that enhanced levels of local leadership, community capacity, social capital, social cohesion, and community capability are themselves important outcomes (regardless of the activity undertaken).[20]

Community development practice in Aotearoa today

Community development practice in Aotearoa today draws on the following principles, derived from national and international literature.

Social Justice

We need to address power imbalances between individuals and between different groups in society. We should place a particular emphasis on promoting the interests of disadvantaged segments of the community, and ideas of respecting and valuing diversity.

The focus should be collective, rather than being based on a response to individual circumstances.

Individual and collective human rights

Good community development practice observes and protects human rights and fundamental freedoms – allowing people to claim their human rights.

Equity

Opportunities and resources should be allocated in an equitable manner to enhance the capacity of all sections of the community to attain their well-being. Discussions of "shared equity" can be progressed in a development phase.

Self-determination and empowerment
Individuals, groups, and communities should be empowered to attain their well-being through collective action. Communities should own and drive the process.

Participation and democracy
Individuals and communities should be active participants, identifying their vision for the future and their needs, and the means of achieving/addressing these. All sections of the community should be effectively engaged. The process and structures should include and empower marginalised and excluded groups within society.

> "Effective participation enables the community to articulate its vision, which enhances the effectiveness and sustainability of development outcomes."[21]

Cooperation/collective action
Community members should work together to identify and undertake action, based on a shared respect for all contributions. Partnerships should be fostered to achieve positive outcomes for all community members.

Action should be based on solidarity with the interests of those experiencing social exclusion.

Sustainability (including, but not exclusively, environmental sustainability)
Social, cultural, economic, and environmental aspects of community should be integrated and balanced. A holistic approach that recognises the connections and interdependencies between different aspects of well-being and the components of communities should be followed.

The needs of both current and future generations should be recognised.

Bi-cultural community development practice in Aotearoa

In addition to the general community development principles set out above, community development practice in Aotearoa must be responsive to the needs and aspirations of Māori communities, and whānau, hapū and iwi groups. The same practice should apply to Pasifika communities.

Munford and Walsh-Tapiata (2006)[22] have identified the following key principles emerging from bicultural community development practice in New Zealand:

- **Having a vision for the future and for what can be achieved** – attempt to identify the dreams of all the populations worked with.

- **Understanding local contexts** – understand communities within their local contexts – different social structures and how these operate culturally within communities. Enable the use of local knowledge to address current challenges.

- **Locating oneself within community** – the need to have a clear understanding of oneself and one's place in the world and how these influence our perspectives.

- **Working within power relations** – need to articulate the nature of power relations and enable communities to redress past wrongs, in order to establish new structures and ways of operating. In Aotearoa, this includes addressing indigenous rights and self-determination.

- **Achieving self-determination** – having one's voice heard and having opportunities for developing knowledge so that participation can be extended and strengthened.

- **Working collectively** – *mahi tahi* – working together towards a common goal.

- **Bringing about positive social change for all communities in Aotearoa** – this incorporates a commitment to overcome challenges that may be faced and requires communities to recognise their ability to effect change.

- **Action and reflection** – reflection requires a review of practices and their impacts in order to learn and adapt. It is important that frameworks are openly debated.

Each principle is applied to suit diverse communities. Perhaps this is a way forward for Pasifika communities to realise their full potential in addressing local issues within their own communities.

Enabling and Building Capacity

Community led principles and practice will develop and help to build capacity within communities. Pasifika communities need to reclaim the customs and traditions that work for them. For example:

> The legend of Kava and its origins comes from the island of Eueiki on the eastern side of Tongatapu where the leprous daughter named Kava sacrificed their daughter as an offering for the Tu'i Tonga (the ancient sacred king). When the Tu'i Tonga heard about the act, he refused the offering but was honoured by their sacrifice. He told them to bury their child and not disturb the ground. After the parents buried the child, two plants sprouted from her grave. The Kava plant at her feet which is bitter and sugar cane at her head which is sweet.[23]

Tongan families use Kava as a way of courtship. Tongan men use taking Kava as a social club, with a Tou'a (woman who serves the Kava). Perhaps women can reclaim their status in Kava as belonging to women equally as men. Perhaps local communities will propose alternative uses of Kava to benefit the local community.

Since that time, Kava has become a significant part of Tongan culture. Kava is symbolic of the land, its people, the culture, and the traditions that they practice. It brings the past into the future and binds them together, meaning that the people cherish their history and their traditions and continue to pass them down to the next generation.

9 – Reflection – Lessons learned

I believe it is vital for Pacific Islanders, and people of other ethnic faiths and diverse traditions, to discover what works for them in expressing their faith and love for their family and the Church, village, and community.

There should always be a balance between giving generously and giving judiciously. Giving within your means is judicious and prudent. Nobody lives with the consequences of giving and your actions except yourself. Therefore, people need to be satisfied with their decisions, which should be made without guilt, pressure, force, or duress.

Easier said than done – I know! But a culturally adept man or woman today should learn both sets of rules and know when to switch between them. This is a principle that I live by in my own life. I am comfortable with both Aotearoa and Tongan cultures, and I switch between the two as the situation demands.

I often move between the two cultures: Aotearoa New Zealand with reference to the Treaty of Waitangi, and Tongan culture when I am associated with my local Tongan Church family or wider Tongan community. I remember preaching during Education week (*Sapate Ako*) on Sunday 20 January 2019, where I delivered my sermon in Tongan and English. I received feedback from both younger and older Tongans about the effectiveness of my sermon to get the message across to young and old. I was glad that my message resonated with the young, and all ages of the Tongan congregation. It was a day to remember, and I enjoyed planning and preparing for the sermon. The full sermon, in Tongan and English is shown in the Appendix. My sermon covered:

The Wine of Transformation: I used this analogy from John 2:11, which explains in the *New International Version*:

> "What Jesus did in Cana of Galilee as the first of his signs through which he revealed his glory; and his disciples believed in him."

Seven key points to remember:

- 'Ulu'aki, 1. 'E malava 'e Sisu o liliu ho mo'ui.
  Jesus… can change your life.

- Ua, 2. 'E malava ae 'Otua ke fetaulaki pe mo koe 'ihe tu'unga 'oku ke 'i ai.
  God can meet you wherever you are in your situation.

- Fika Tolu, 3. 'E malava e Sisu ke fakafonu ho mo'ui ke fonu ngutungutu 'ihe lelei taha.
  Jesus can fulfil your life to the brim with his blessings.

- Fika Fa, 4. Pe'a faka haa'i e Sisu 'ene mafimafi o tau tui kiai.
  Jesus manifested his glory so that we can believe in him!

- Fika Nima, 5. 'E malava ke faka tau'ataina'i kitautolu 'e he Laumalie Ma'oni'oni.
  We can be truly transformed through the gift of the Holy Spirit.

- Fika Ono, 6. 'E malava ke tau nofo ma'u 'iate ia 'ihe 'ene Kelesi.
  We can remain transformed in Him through His Unconditional Grace, Love and Mercy.

- Fika Fitu 7. Ko Sisu pe koe Hala, moe Mo'oni mo e Mo'ui.
  Jesus is the only way, the truth and light for our Salvation.

Living within your means can be difficult within Pasifika culture if you have a church role or village responsibilities such as a (*Matai, Matapule, Faifekau* or *Faifeau*).

I believe the key to managing the pressures and demands in Pasifika communities is to prioritise the duties and responsibilities in order of significance. For example, serving God and the Church is just as important as being there for your family, village, and community.

Being disciplined with your money is important. One needs to be careful when making financial decisions to not go outside one's own financial comfort level. We need to refrain from offering more than we can afford or are capable of giving. We need to have clear financial goals and work towards them in a disciplined way. Saying 'no' is frowned upon in Pasifika culture, as noted in Tana Umaga's situation. However, knowing when to say 'no' is better than making careless choices, falling into debt, and putting yourself in a financial predicament.

I looked at how the Church recognises Pasifika culture and traditions and also its place in the secular state system. There is a need to recognise a framework for Pasifika culture and traditions in the Church and secular state system. There should be a platform for the recognition of other cultures across Aotearoa, reflecting our changing demographics and growing diversity. We need to identify the pressures and strains people live with, and be ready to provide for early Church, state, and social interventions.

Learning from our situations

Let's take the example of the Blues and North Harbour prop Michael Tamoaieta who died (Rest in Love).

There were signs that nobody knew about or could talk about. Blues Chief Executive Michael Redman said the Blues were stunned by the news and deeply saddened at his death. There were questions for the Blues and North Harbour organisations about what they could do to provide mechanisms of support and transition for Pasifika rugby players. This remains a work-in-progress.

I commend the effort and actions of Johnny Tuivasa-Sheck who retired from playing in the NRL. Johnny explained the pressures he grew up with as a sports prodigy.

In an article appearing on the Stuff news website in 2019,[24] Johnny Tuivasa-Sheck, brother of Warriors skipper Roger Tuivasa-Sheck, admitted, when he announced his NRL retirement, that playing in the NRL was never really something he truly wanted. Tuivasa-Sheck, or JTS as he is known to his thousands of social media followers, opened up on the pressures of growing up as a rugby league prodigy in a video titled "You were supposed to be the greatest rugby player anyone has ever seen."[25] It was published on YouTube and shared across social media, along with a message in the description where the 23 year old, officially announced he was giving the game away.

Speaking up, saying 'no' and setting the record straight takes courage and JTS did just that. He touched on the pressures of Samoan boys growing up in Aotearoa, his father's expectations, and the problem of being labelled "a rugby player" by those around him from an early age, without ever being asked if that was what he wanted to do.

Parents, family, extended family, Pasifika churches, and villages can expect a lot, putting unnecessary pressure, demands, stress and strain on young athletes. However, JTS reminded us that knowing yourself, and what you are capable of doing or becoming, should be how we measure an individual's success.

JTS's powerful piece has drawn attention and praise from many, both inside and outside rugby league circles. JTS's experience about being boxed into the rugby player role at age 14 and never truly having the courage to pursue another path speaks volumes for other Pasifika athletes.

Finding your own voice and pathway in life

Knowing yourself and being true to who you are is the key to finding your own voice and pathway in life. Finding an effective way to communicate this to the people you love is vitally important. Demanding respect, space, and privacy when you need it is equally important. You need to be comfortable with yourself and your actions and take time to educate your family and make them understand why you have made your decision and taken a different path in life to the one they expected.

Epistemology of Pasifika People – Native Common Sense

Understanding the epistemology of Pasifika people is important for understanding their native common sense and use of sarcasm. The knowledge of Pasifika people is embedded in their culture. To understand the worldviews of Pasifika people, researchers need to study the knowledge that is revealed in the lives of the people. Researchers need to take account of the Pasifika habits of movement, likes and dislikes, to get closer to understanding why pacific people behave the way they do.

> Knowledge is embedded in the culture of the people.
> Knowledge comes through in the lives of the people.
>
> *Una Nabobo-Baba, Fijian*

Hidden Meaning and Interpretation – Pasifika use of Sarcasm

Understanding the use by Pasifika people of sarcasm, metaphors, and nuances, and correctly interpreting cultural behaviour in social gatherings, is necessary to unravel the hidden meanings in what they say. In formal gatherings, there is a shift from the everyday language to a metaphorical level of communication called sarcasm. This creates additional challenges, as considerable insider knowledge is required to correctly interpret the use of sarcasm by Pasifika people.

In a Pasifika context sarcasm involves saying one thing but meaning another, which requires skill based on cultural knowledge to carry out successfully. Pasifika sarcasm uses metaphor and has multiple layers of meaning. It is developed by skirting around a sensitive subject and approaching it repeatedly from different points of view.

Non-Pasifika people, who are unaware of these nuances and ways of speaking, can easily misunderstand what Pasifika people really mean by what they are saying. Decoding hidden meanings and unravelling them layer-by-layer until they can be understood, requires considerable creative skill, patience, and imagination.

We need to unpack Pasifika sarcasm, metaphors, and nuances, and interpret *heliaki*[26] used by people in social gatherings. For example, in the Tongan context when a person says they are fine or *sai pe*,[27] it doesn't always mean they are fine. Instead, they say they are fine as a cover up for how they are really feeling. In some instances of Pasifika suicide this could have been the situation and we need to find solutions, answers, resolve, mechanisms, and measures for understanding Pasifika sarcasm.

Unbroken – To know we belong

Three phrases sum up three important messages:

Compassion and Forgiveness – To love our neighbour as our self.

Hospitality and Generosity – To welcome all people.

Community and Identity – To know we belong.

The concept of 'Unbroken' derives from the 2014 war film produced and directed by Angelina Jolie and written by the Coen brothers, Richard LaGravenese, and William Nicholson. It is based on the 2010 non-fiction book by Laura Hillenbrand, *Unbroken: A World War II Story of Survival, Resilience, and Redemption*. The film and the book emphasise the will power to survive through mental toughness, physical strength, and resilience.

The same applies to the mana and *tāpuaki*[28] of Pasifika people "to know that they have a place and belonging in Aotearoa." Pacific people have much to offer in spirit, faith, culture, intellect, education, arts and crafts, cuisine, music, sports, and the list is not exhaustive. Pasifika people have a shared equity in Aotearoa as our adopted home 'to know we belong,' and create a pathway to redemption.

Placemaking For Redemption – Making something better and more acceptable

Placemaking for redemption is the act of making something better or more acceptable. Placemaking is an approach where people work together to make places better, not only for themselves but for others and for the place itself. Placemaking is inclusive and participatory. It helps people grow aroha, connection to each other and to our places of identify. It forges strong kaupapa, identity, belonging and meaning. It values local knowledge and the lived experiences of everyday people as much as experts.[29] Placemaking inspires people to collectively reimagine and reinvent their public spaces by strengthening connections through a shared collaborative process that capitalises on local assets, strengths, goals, potential aspirations, and opportunities.[30]

The art of qualitative *talanoa* or exploration of the views, perceptions, realities, and experiences of Pasifika people living in Aotearoa can best be captured in the relational space of those communities. It's a process of democratising, so that everyone in a neighbourhood benefits when a place is improved. Involving local people in decision making for their local places uplifts the mana of communities, to make them stronger and healthier: environmentally, culturally, socially, and economically.[31]

Learning by Doing and Empowerment

We learn by doing. Community building and restoration relies on the active involvement of local citizens in decisions and actions related to 'their place.' All communities have strengths and assets on which foundations for successful community development can be built, especially when existing resources are used differently to create new opportunities. Some communities have the experience and capacity to lead together, while others require support to strengthen their communities, gather local voices and be a catalyst for action. This learning by doing will generate confidence within communities that they can 'get things done' for themselves and with the help of others.

Strategies for building community resilience are useful in times of crisis, in responding to everyday opportunities and challenges, and for gearing communities for change yet to come. Community building approaches focus on growing social capital by intentionally encouraging community cohesion and senses of identity, connection, pride, and place.[32] These principles can be applied by Pasifika people, wherever they are today in their place and communities, to make the necessary steps for change.

Conclusion

Parents, families, churches, communities, sports organisations, villages, society, and government – all have a role to play in ensuring that there are proper mechanisms and support systems in place to support, guide, manage and monitor the pressures, strains and demands on Pasifika people, or anyone from an ethnically diverse background living in Aotearoa.

We saw how Aotearoa responded to the 2019 mosque shootings in Christchurch, where 51 lives were lost. People demanded answers and action to ensure the safety and security of our ethnic communities.

Calls for health and safety, well-being and security measures are more prevalent now, especially during the current COVID-19 pandemic, than ever before. Our society demands tolerance, acceptance and understanding of all races and cultures.

So too, we should demand a better understanding of the pressures and strains on Pasifika families living in Aotearoa, from churches, sports organisations, communities, workplaces, institutions, society, and advocate for the enactment of laws and regulations that make the changes necessary to aid and support Pasifika people living in Aotearoa.

Appendix

Sermon delivered by Rubinstine Manukia on Sunday 20 January 2019 at Pulela'a New Lynn Tongan Methodist Church

———◆———

Koe Kaveinga 'eku Malanga:

"Ko E Uaine 'O E Liliu."

Veesi Malanga: Sione 2:11

Na'e fai 'eni 'e Sisū 'i Kena 'i Kaleli, ko e 'uluaki 'o 'ene ngaahimana, pea ne fakae'a ai hono langilangi; pea na'e tui pikitai kiate ia 'ene kau ako.

My sermon is about the:

"Wine of Transformation." I use this analogy from the Book of John 2:11, which explains in the International Version:

"What Jesus did in Cana of Galilee as the first of his signs through which he revealed his glory; and his disciples believed in him."

'Oku 'iai ae ngaahi me'a lalahi e 7 teu fakamamafa:

There are 7 things that I will emphasise that I want you to remember:

'Ulu'aki, 1. 'E malava 'e Sisu o liliu ho mo'ui – Number 1, Jesus… can change your life.

Ko e Kosipeli 'o e 'aho ni, ko e talanoa ia ki he 'uluaki mana 'a Sisu he'ene liliu 'ae vai ko e Uaine, he ta'ane na'e fai 'i Kena 'o Kaleli. Koe talanoa maheni 'eni. Ko Kena ko e ki'i kolo si'isi'i, pea ko e mali ko 'eni na'e katoa ki ai 'a e ki'i komiuniti. Ko e kakai kotoa 'o e ki'i kolo na'e 'i ai, maheni mo e famili mei he ngaahi kolo kaunga'api, hange ko Nasaleti, ko ia na'e 'i ai mo Sisu, 'ene fa'e ko Mele pea mo e ni'ihi 'o e kau ako.

Na'e faka'ofo'ofa ae mali pea nau fiefia, kae faka'ohovale kuo ta'ofia 'a e katoanga he kuo maha 'a e Uaine. 'I he ngaahi 'aho ko ia 'o Sisu, ka maha pe si'isi'i 'a e Uaine, pea 'oku fakamā pea hange 'oku ta'etoka'i 'a e kau fakaafe. Pea 'oku fa'a lava pe ia 'e he taimi 'e ni'ihi ke faka'ilo 'e he kau fakaafe 'a e taha 'oku 'a'ana 'a e katoanga koe'uhi ko 'ene si'i 'a e Uaine. Ko e ta'efaka'apa'apa lahi ia ki he kau fakaafe ka nounou 'a e Uaine. Ko ia 'oku 'i he tu'unga fakatu'utamaki 'a e ki'i famili ni fakasosiale, pea mo fakalao he nounou 'a e Uaine.

'I he nounou 'a e Uaine, ko e taimi ia na'e hanga ai 'a Mele kia Sisu, o ne lea " Kuo 'osi 'enau Uaine." Mary turned to Jesus and said, "The banquet has run out of wine!"

Tau sio loto pe kihe 'etau ngaahi katoanga he 'ahoni. 'Kapau e si'i ae me'a tokoni pe 'inu, kuo tau 'iha tu'unga fakatu'utamaki pe fakamaa. Koe 'u hia he 'oku tau tokanga kihe sio mai ae kakai pea moe 'a takai.

Pea 'oku tau fa'a pehe pe he taimi lahi ki hotau 'Otua. 'Oku tau toki hanga pe kihe 'Otua he taimi 'oku tau maha ai pe nounou 'i ha me'a. 'Oku tau hanga kihe 'Otua 'i he 'osi hoatu ivi, pe hala he pa'anga, ae taimi 'oku 'ikai ke tau toe 'ilo'i ai 'a e me'a ke fai. Pe ko 'etau toki hanga pe ki he 'Otua he taimi 'oku teu ai 'etau ngaahi sivi he 'ako.

Taimi 'oku 'ikai ai ha'a tau 'amanaki, pea mo e ha fua 'a e ngaahi palopalema 'o e mo'ui. Tau toki hanga pe ki he 'Otua he'etau 'ilo'i 'oku tau fiema'u 'ene tokoni.

Ua, 2. 'E malava ae 'Otua ke fetaulaki pe mo koe 'ihe tu'unga 'oku ke 'i ai – Number 2, God can meet you wherever you are in your situation.

Ko e ongoongo lelei 'o e Kosipeli 'o e 'aho ni, 'oku lava 'e he 'Otua kene fetaulaki mo kitautolu he me'a 'oku tau maha mo nounou ai. Na'a mo 'etau ako 'oku ne malava ke fakafonu kitautolu. 'Oku malava 'e he 'Otua kene fetaulaki mo kitautolu 'i he ngaahi feitu'u 'oku tau fiema'u ai.

Think of a time when you were in a crisis or in a difficult situation. When you were at your weakest… lowest point, or in your darkest hour or moment. Who was there for you? John tells us that God can meet us in our time of need. That we can have the hope and belief that God will always be there and that he will never forsake us!

Pe a ko e me'a ia na'e fai 'e he 'Eiki he taane ko 'eni. He fakaha na'e fai 'e Mele kia Siau, kuo 'osi 'enau Uaine. Pea tali 'e Sisu "He ko e ha Fine'eiki 'eta kaunga ki ai? Jesus replied to Mary what is our involvement in this? 'Oku te'eki ke hoko mai hoku taimi." My time has not yet come or arrived? Hange 'oku 'ikai ke faka'apa'apa'i 'e Sisu 'a 'ene Fa'e he tali na'ane fai.

Ko hono mo'oni 'oku 'ikai pehe na'e ta'e tokanga 'a Sisu ki he lea 'ene Fa'e mo e 'osi 'a e Uaine, ka na'ane 'ilo'i 'oku 'ikai ko e 'uhinga ia 'o 'ene hoko mai ki mamani. Jesus knew that this was not the reason why he came to earth incarnation.

'Oku tau 'ilo'i na'e tokanga 'a Sisu ki he nounou 'a e Uaine koe'uhi he na'e 'ikai tene tali, Sai 'aupito, 'ene maha 'a e Uaine. Pe kene pehe 'oku 'ikai totonu ke mou inu Uaine koe'uhi he 'oku kovi ia. Na'e 'ikai tene tafulu'i 'a e famili he 'ikai palani lelei 'enau ki'i mali. Pe ko ha'ane ngaahi'i 'a e kau fakaafe he fu'u inu lahi fakavalevale pehe.

Jesus knew he had to do something. He kuo pau kene fai ha me'a. Na'e 'osi 'ilo'i ia 'e Mele, he neongo 'a e tali na'e fai 'e Sisu ki ai, ka na'e tala 'e Mele ia ki he kau ngaue, "Mou fai e me'a kotoa 'e tala atu 'e Sisu." Do whatever Jesus asks you to do. Pea ne fai ki ai 'a e kau ngaue, he 'oku talamai 'e Sione na'a nau fakafonu 'a e ngaahi hina. Ne fekau e Sisu ke fakafonu vai ae ngaahi 'Angavai Maka 'e 'Ono, na'e tuku ai koe 'uhi koe fakama'a faka-Siu.

Imagine kapau te tau fai ha me'a 'e fepaki pe contradictory moe tau 'ulunga anga fakafonua, 'e hoko ia koe talangata'a. Ka 'oku faka mahino mai e Sione ne ha'u a Sisu ia o fakakakato 'etau to nounou. "Jesus came on earth to fulfil the scriptures and all our shortfalls in life" Ke tau tokanga na 'oku tau faka mu'amu'a 'ange 'e kitautolu 'etau 'ulunga anga fakafonua, 'ouau faka lotu, 'e tau tokanga kihe sio mai ae kakai, pea mo 'etau vaa moe tangata 'iate ia mo 'ene mo'oni! God's truth must prevail over everything and all else!

Fika Tolu, 3. 'E malava e Sisu ke fakafonu ho mo'ui ke fonu ngutungutu 'ihe lelei taha. Number 3, Jesus can fulfil your life to the brim with his blessings.

Ne fekau 'e Sisu ke 'ave ae ngaahi hina, kihe matapule 'oku fai tu'utu'u ni he mali. Fakatonga ange na'e fonu ngutungutu ae ngaahi hina. Pea 'oku tatau pe ia moe 'ofa ae 'Otua ma'a kitautolu, 'oku fonu ngutungutu 'ene 'ofa, pea 'oku ne fo'aki ae lelei taha ma'a kitautolu. What an awesome God that loves us unconditionally despite our unworthiness!

Pea 'i he 'ahi'ahi'i 'e he matapule e vai, kuo liliu 'o Uaine, na'e 'ohovale ae Matapule ia, he 'oku 'ikai ko ha Uaine ma'ama'a, ka ko e lelei taha 'o e Uaine. The master of ceremonies was surprised that the wine left to last was the very best and finest of wines!

You might be thinking how can water turn to wine, and I know the kids here are probably thinking the same?

But don't be confused when you hear water is turned to wine. It's used as an example of the transformation of life, from old to new, meihe motu'a kihe fo'ou, pe koe liliu oe mou'i.

Fika Fa, 4. Pe'a faka haa'i e Sisu 'ene mafimafi o tau tui kiai. Number 4. Jesus manifested his glory so that we can believe in him!

Ko ia 'i he tu'unga fakatu'utamaki na'e 'i ai 'a e ongo me'a mali he nounou 'o e Uaine pea mo hona fakamaa'i, The situation turned into a blessing, ko 'eni kuo fai hona fakamalo'ia'i mo fakahikihiki'i he 'ena 'ave fakamuimui 'a e Uaine lelei taha. It's often that we give the very best first, but Jesus said whoever wants to be first will be last and those that are last will be first. Ke tau toe mo'ui faka'aki'aki mui ange mo fakatokilalo. Pea tau 'ofa mo'oni he masiva moe faka'ofa. This is symbolic of Jesus who lives in the humble and meek at heart and does not favour in the proud and boastful.

Ko e Uaine 'o e liliu. Ko Sisu ia 'oku ne liliu 'a e vai ki he Uaine lelei taha 'oku 'ikai ke tau 'ilo ki ai. 'Oku fakahoko 'eni 'e Sisu he 'oku ne tokanga mai ki he 'etau mo'ui. 'Oku tokanga mai 'a e 'Otua ki he me'a kotoa pe 'o 'etau mo'ui, he 'oku ne 'ilo'i 'a e lou'ulu kotoa pe hotau 'ulu. God knows us and he knows our destinies even before we are born.

Fakakaukau ange ki ho'o mo'ui he taimi ni, koe ha me'a 'oku ke hoha'a mo tokanga ki ai? 'Oku fefe ho mo'ui fakalaumalie, pea kuo ke tali mo'oni ae 'Otua kiho mo'ui? Kapau te tau lau ae sekoni, miniti, houa, 'aho, uike, mahina pe moe ta'u 'oku tau ma'u lotu ai, kuo 'osi taimi ke tau hu kitautolu ki hevani. Ka 'oku pehe koa e Pulela'a? Toe tokanga ange na 'oku nge'esi pe 'etau lotu. Ka ko kita pe te ke 'ilo kiai.

Tau sio ange kihe 'etau to'onga mo'ui, do our actions portray what we say... are our actions the same as our lip service? If we are Christian, then why do we have jealousy and animosity in our hearts? Kapau koe Kalisitiane mo'oni kitautolu koe ha e me'a 'oku tau kei fehi'a ai ki ho tau kaunga'api, pe sio lalo, pe loto kovi kiha taha moe ha fua oe ngaahi palaku oe mo'ui? When we look in the mirror, we can see our true reflection.

Fika Nima, 5. 'E malava ke faka tau'ataina'i kitautolu 'e he Laumalie Ma'oni'oni. Number 5, We can be truly transformed through the gift of the Holy Spirit.

Siasi 'oku 'ikai ko e talanoa 'o e 'aho ni ko e liliu pe 'o e vai ke Uaine, ka 'oku toe hulu atu. 'Oku tala 'e Sione na'e fakahoko 'e Sisu 'ene 'uluaki mana 'i Kena 'o Kaleli, pea ha ai hono lāngilangi.

'Oku ha 'a e fo'i mana 'e 7 'a Sisu he tohi 'a Sione ko e ngaahi mana ne fakaha ai hono lāngilangi 'ia Sisu Kalaisi. 'Oku ne fakahaa'i ko Sisu 'oku 'ikai ko e faiako pe, pe ko e palofita, ka ko Sisu Kalaisi koe 'alo ia 'o e 'Otua, ko e Misaia ia ko e fakamo'ui 'o mamani. 'Oku fakahaa'i ia he talateu 'o e Kosiepli, kuo hoko 'a folofola 'o kakano, 'o ne 'afio 'i hotau lotolotonga. Ko e 'Otua ia 'iate kitautolu. Through the gift of the holy spirit we can receive Jesus and be truly transformed… and know that God is truly with us!

Na'ane fakahaa'i 'ene Kelesi 'ihe lalahi ae 'utu 'a e vai ki he hina 'e 6 taki lita 'e 100. Ko e fu'u lita ia 'e 600 'oku fakama'a 'aki 'a e va'e oe kakai Siu 'i he 'ao 'o e 'Otua he 'enau ouau.

Na'e fakafonu 'e Sisu 'a e ngaahi fu'u hina tatau 'i he Uaine, ko e lelei taha, ko e me'a'ofa ta'etotongi ki he kakai na'a nau 'i he tu'unga kuo nau maha. 'E lava ketau pehe kuo liliu 'e Sisu 'a e vai 'o e lao ki he Uaine 'o e Kelesi? Pea mooni pe 'a Sione vahe 1:17 "Ko Mosese na'ane tuku mai e Lao, 'a e 'Otua. Ka kuo fakafou mai 'ia Sisu Kalaisi 'a 'ene 'ofa tu'unga'a mo e mo'oni."

Fika Ono, 6. 'E malava ke tau nofo ma'u 'iate ia 'ihe 'ene Kelesi. Number 6, We can remain transformed in Him through His Unconditional Grace, Love and Mercy

Siasi na'e hoko mai 'a Sisu 'o kumi 'a e masiva, ae fie inu a moe fie kai ia, mo kinautolu 'oku fie mo'ui, pea kene ha'iha'i 'a e lavelavea pea ke foaki 'a e mo'ui mo fakafoki kitautolu kihe 'Otua.

Mahalo pe ko 'etau mo'ui 'oku fonu ngutungutu he 'etau ngaahi tukufakaholo ouau 'o e mo'ui, he 'etau pehe te tau ngaue'i pe hotau fakamo'ui pea tau va lelei ai mo hotau 'Otua, Ka he 'ikai ngaue ia.

Ko e taimi 'o 'etau maha 'oku 'ikai fiema'u ai 'a e ngaahi ouau tukufakaholo ia 'o e lotu, ka 'oku tau fiema'u kitautolu 'a e Kelesi 'a e 'Otua. We should be yearning for God's forgiveness, grace, and mercy. 'Oku 'ikai ke tau fiema'u ha vai, ka 'oku tau fiema'u 'a e Uaine 'o e Kelesi. We seek God's change and transformation for our lives, like water turned to fine wine.

Taimi 'e ni'ihi 'oku tau fiema'u ke tau laka kimu'a he mo'ui pea tau pāfua ha fu'u holisi, pea 'oku tau holomui 'o toe laka atu he hala kehe, 'o tau toe fa'aki pe he fu'u holisi 'e taha, pea ko hotau 'atunga pe 'e. We are creatures of habit and Scientists say that it normally takes 21 days to break a habit if we stick to it, but it could take a lifetime. 'Oku fa'a hoko 'eni he nofo famili, ngaue pea toe hoko pe he loto Siasi. 'Oku lahi ange ae politikale he Siasi he parliament lahi!

Siasi, 'oku hoko mai ae ta'u fo'ou 'oku tau fokotu'utu'u fo'ou, ke kamata fo'ou pea tau fononga atu, pe kuo tau hela'ia, pea 'afe 'o maha 'a e mo'ui he feinga, pea tau fo'i ai pe. Ko e ngaahi taimi pehe 'oku tau fiema'u 'a e Kelesi 'a e 'Otua. Neongo 'ene tatapuni 'a e ngaahi hala 'oku tau fononga ai. Ko e hala pe taha 'oku lava ke tau hao ai, and that's the long and narrow path which Jesus conquered and a challenge for us.

Fika Fitu 7. Ko Sisu pe koe Hala, moe Mo'oni mo e Mo'ui. Number 7, Jesus IS the only way, the truth and light for our Salvation.

Manatu'i 'a e lea 'a Sisu ki he 'ene Fa'e he kole na'ane fai? "He ko e ha Fine'eiki 'eta kaunga ki ai? 'Osi 'a e ngaahi ta'u meihe liliu 'e Sisu 'a e vai ke Uaine, na'e hoko mai taimi 'o Sisu. Hili 'ene ha'ele fakatu'i ki Selusalema, na'e tala 'e Sisu kihe 'ene kau ako kuo hoko mai hono taimi ke fakalangilangi'i 'a e foha 'o e tangata. Pea 'i he efiafi hifo 'o e pasiona mo 'ene pekia he Kolosi na'e lotu ai 'a Sisu. 'E Tamai fakalangilangi ā ho Foha, kae fakalāngilangi'i koe 'e ho Foha."

'Osi 'a e ngaahi ta'u meihe liliu 'e Sisu 'a e vai ko e Uaine, na'e toe lea ai 'a Sisu ki he 'ene Fa'e, "Fefine ko 'ena ho'o Tama." Taimi na'e liliu ai 'e Sisu 'a e vai ki he Uaine, na'ane fakahaa'i si'isi'i pe hono langilangi, ka 'i he 'ene pekia he kolosi, na'ane fakahaa'i kakato ai 'ene mafimafi.

Fakatokanga'i 'i he hili hono liliu 'e Sisu 'a e vai ko e Uaine na'e fēfē 'a e kau ako? Talamai 'e Sione na'e tui 'ene kau ako kiate ia. Ko e tui kia Sisu ko e kaveinga mahu'inga ia he kosipeli 'a Sione. Pea 'oku fiema'u kitautolu Fanau 'ako ke tau tui kia Sisu he ako 'oku tau fai.

Fēfē Koe? 'Oku ke Tui? Vakai na'a 'oku 'i ai ha 'elia ho'o mo'ui he 'aho ni 'oku maha ai 'a e Uaine. Vakai'i na'a kuo maha 'a e MAKA ho'o mo'ui, pea 'ikai kei lava keke laka atu ki mu'a 'i ho ivi pe tokotaha?

Fanau 'ako 'oku ke fo'i he ako, pe fakapikopiko, pe 'oku ke HE ho moui? 'Oku lava 'e Sisu ke liliu koe, keke malohi he 'ako, pea ke fakatonutonu ho'o mo'ui.

'I he liliu 'e Sisu 'a e vai ko e Uaine, 'oku tau sio ai ki he fakafetaulaki 'oku fai 'e he 'Otua ma'a kitautolu 'i he ngaahi feitu'u 'oku tau maha ai, ke liliu 'etau mo'ui mei he tauhi 'o e lao, ki he 'ene Kelesi.

Fanau 'ako ko e ta'u ni tau fakaafe'i 'a e Uaine lelei taha ko Sisu Kalaisi, ketau inu ai pea kene fakafo'ou kitautolu he 'etau tokanga ki he ako. Hange pe ko e hoko mai 'a e 'ilo ki hotau 'atamai 'o liliu kitautolu meihe vale ke tau poto.

'Oku pehe pe 'a e hoko mai 'a e Uiane fo'ou mo lelei taha, ko Sisu Kalaisi, 'o ne fakafonu mo liliu kitautolu meihe 'etau maha o fonu. Ko e mana 'o e 'aho ni, 'oku ne taki mo tuhu'i kitautolu ki he Kolosi, 'a ia na'e pekia ai 'a Sisu kene liliu 'a e vai ko e Uaine, pea kene liliu ai, 'a e 'ikai ha 'amanaki ki ha 'amanaki, pe liliu ai 'a e angahala ki he haohaoa, pea moe mate ki he mo'ui.

Kapau te tau sio ki he kamata 'o e Kosipeli 'o e 'aho ni 'oku lava ketau 'ilo'i ai na'e hoko 'a e mana ko 'eni 'i he 'aho hono tolu. Pea ko hono mo'oni ko e pekia 'a Sisu 'oku 'ikai ko e ngata'anga ia 'o e talanoa, he na'ane toetu'u mai 'i hono 'aho tolu.

Pea 'oku 'ikai ke ngata pe ai, ka 'i Hevani te tau kau ai ki he katoanga 'o e mali 'a e 'Eiki ta'ane. Sisu Kalaisi mo hono Uaifi ko e Siasi. Pea 'e lahi mo hulu atu hono Uaine.

Ko e 'aho ni 'oku tau hange kotoa pe ko Mele, 'oku tau 'ilo'i 'oku taha pe 'a e tokotaha ke tau tafoki ki ai he taimi 'oku tau maha ai he Uaine. Mahalo pe ko e 'aho ni 'oku fiema'u 'e he 'Otua kene fakafonu koe ki he ngutungutu 'aki 'ene Uaine 'o 'ene Kelesi. Pea mahalo pe ko e 'aho ni kuo ke fakamo'oni'i 'i ho'o mo'ui teke tui mo tali mo'oni ae 'Eiki kiho mo'ui. Ko e Uaine ia 'o e Liliu tene liliu koe he aho ni, mo e ta'u ni.

Talamonu atu ke mou ma'u ha feinga 'ako monu'ia mo Kelesi'ia. Pea ke manatu'i koe tufa talenti 'oku 'ia Kalaisi 'ihe apasia mo'oni. Ha ia 'ia 1 Kolonito Vahe 12 (lesoni tolu oe 'ahoni) ae tufa taleniti.

Kiate au koe 'ako mahu'inga, koha 'ako 'oku 'aonga ke fo'aki ae mo'ui ke me'a ngaue'aki 'e he 'Eiki (kc fakamu'amu'a ma'u pe ae 'Otua 'ihe me'a kotoa pe), 2, Koha 'ako 'oku aonga pe 'ground breaking' hono taumu'a, maae Fonua, Sosaieti, Komuiniti, Famili pe mo kita foki.

Ko 'eku 'ako he Lao, ko 'eku fekumi kiha fakama'opo'opo, balance, pe middle ground, maae ngaahi fepakipaki fakalao, ae Lao oe Fonua (Law of the Land), Lao ae Siasi (Methodist Church Law), pea moe 'etau Tui Fakakalisitiane moe 'ulunga'anga Fakafonua, (I explored the clashes and tensions that arise in the search for a reconciliation of the differences in ecclesiastic law, secular law and our cultural beliefs and identity). Koha fekumi kiha fo'unga ke faka'ilonga'i 'aki 'etau Tui fakakalisitiane moe 'ulunga'anga fakafonua 'ihe lao 'oe Fonuani, (ke 'iai ha tau le'o he fonuani), pea moha fakahinohino 'i he lao 'oe Siasi. Koha 'ako e 'aonga ae 'findings of my research' kiate kitautolu fakalokufua as an aggregate, pea moe Kaha'u 'oe Siasi.

Ketau manatu'i he taimi 'o e maha 'etau ngaahi feinga 'ako, ketau tafoki kia Sisu ka ne fakafonu koe pea mo au, 'aki 'ene Kelesi mo 'ene poto faka 'Otua (We ask God to fill us with His Holy Wisdom), moe 'ene poto Fakapotopoto (and His Common Sense not ours), pea ketau tui ai kiate ia!

Tuku 'a e Uaine Lelei taha ko Sisu Kalaisi (We ask for the simplicity and purity of Christ to change us) kene liliu'i ho mo'ui, keke hoko koha tokotaha fo'ou, pe ke lave o fakamo'oni mo fai 'ene finangalo i mamani.

Pea 'oku fiema'u lahi ha kau 'Ako Mohu Founga Fakapotopoto, pe Pioneer, We need Future Thinkers, Innovators of Change and Transformation, to find cures, answers and solutions for the issues and challenges that we face today, and more importantly, Visionaries for a Vision for the Future.

'Emeni.

Endnotes

1. http://www.methodist.org.nz/administration_division/mcnz_law_book
2. https://www.stuff.co.nz/sport/rugby/75254050/polynesian-athletes-face-stresses-and-strains-in-order-to-give-back-to-families
3. Tana Umaga and Paul Thomas, *Tana Umaga: Up Close* (Auckland: Hodder Moa, 2007)
4. https://www.education.govt.nz/assets/Documents/Early-Childhood/Play-ideas/Play-ideas-complete-collection.pdf
5. https://www.education.govt.nz/
6. https://faithandwork.princeton.edu/research/integration-profile
7. https://www.researchgate.net/publication/254097594_Connecting_religion_and_work_Patterns_and_influences_of_work-faith_integration
8. https://edspace.american.edu/theworldmind/2016/04/01/the-u-s-and-legal-pluralism-reckoning-private-rights-with-the-public/
9. Mabon v Conference of the Methodist Church of New Zealand - [1998] 3 NZLR 513
10. Palu v Conference of the Methodist Church of New Zealand (2003) 1 NZTR 13-008 (HC)
11. Doe, Norman (2013), Cambridge University Press, DOI https://doi.org/10.1017/CBO9781139021906
12. *Like a Dove: A memoir and biography in honour of Sione Tavo Manukia*. Rubinstine Manukia. Philip Garside Publishing Ltd (2016). https://pgpl.co.nz/ebooks/like-a-dove-ebook/
13. *Fisi'inaua 'i Vaha – A Tongan Migrant's Way: A Methodist Minister Applies Tongan Social Concepts in a New Zealand Setting*. Siosifa Pole. Philip Garside Publishing Ltd (2016). https://pgpl.co.nz/print-books/fisiinaua-i-vaha-a-tongan-migrants-way-print/
14. L. Chile "The historical context of community development in Aotearoa New Zealand", *Community Development Journal Vol.41 (4)*, (October 2006) p. 411.
15. ibid p. 415.
16. ibid. pp. 407-425
17. ibid (2006) p.423.
18. ibid (2006) p.425.
19. The Reducing Inequalities Strategy sought to: build the capacity of disadvantaged communities, beginning with Māori and Pacific communities; support local level solutions developed by community groups; and strengthen existing programmes delivered by government agencies.
20. The results from the CCI initiatives in the USA suggest that less tangible outcomes such as "social capital" still need to have intentional strategies to achieve them, rather than hoping they will be a by-product of other strategies. (See International review paper)

21 L. Chile (2007) *Community Development Practice in New Zealand: Exploring Good Practice*. Institute of Public Policy and Auckland University of Technology, p. 25.
22. R. Munford and W. Walsh-Tapiata, "Community development: working in the bicultural context of Aotearoa New Zealand" *Community Development Journal, Special Issue: Community Development Practice in a bicultural context: Aotearoa New Zealand. Vol. 41 (4)*, October 2006.
23. https://www.themanaacademy.org/post/tongan-language-culture-taumafa-kava#:~:text=When%20the%20Tu'i%20Tonga,and%20not%20disturb%20the%20ground.
24. https://www.stuff.co.nz/sport/league/110332777/jts-retires-from-nrl-talks-of-pressures-growing-up-as-a-sports-prodigy
25. https://youtu.be/_NgaR2JAbZ4
26. Sarcasm in Tongan, means to talanoa, speak ironically, or to say one thing and mean another.
27. Means 'fine' in Tongan. To be good, good enough, unobjectionable, all right, to be good or suitable, to be in good or reasonably good condition, to be well, just as well, advisable, a good thing, to be acceptable or permissible, to be beneficial.
28. In Tongan it means blessing. To pronounce blessing. An act of blessing or good thing, benefit, advantage, regarded as a blessing.
29 See information available at https://inspiringcommunities.org.nz/ and https://www.communitythink.nz/
30 https://www.pps.org/article/what-is-placemaking
31 https://www.placemaking.nz/what-is-placemaking
32 *Learning by doing Community-Led Change in Aotearoa NZ*, (2013), Inspiring Communities, ISBN 9780473244200

Index

Scripture
Genesis 1:1-2:2 26
Genesis 1:26-27 27
Genesis 2:7 27
Genesis 2:24 26
Genesis 9:5-6 27
Exodus 20:8 26
Exodus 20:13 27
Job 34:14-15 27
Psalm 139 26
Matthew 22:36-40 17
Mark 12:17 34
John 2:11 46
Romans 13:1-7 27

A
Anglican Church in Aotearoa 32
Aotearoa, constitutional framework of 24, 32

C
Chile, L. 40
Church
    as a village 29
    ideal role of 16
Church and State
    separation between 26
    State should consult with churches 34
Church Law, formal recognition of 34
community development
    bi-cultural practice of 43
    capacity, enabling and building 44
    principles of 40
COVID-19 Lockdowns 20
cultural competence
    in government agencies 37

D
depression
    diagnosis of in Pasifika people 27

F
Fa'alavelave, Samoan tradition of 11
Fakame, White Sunday celebration for children 5
Fetokoni'aki, Tongan tradition of 11
Fotuaika, Mosese 12
Freedom of Association 30

G
giving
    concepts of 9
    demands on Pasifika professionals 11
    personal commitment to 22
    public perception of 16
    refusing requests for 22
    should be willing, without pressure 22

H
human rights, individual and collective 42

I
iwi based justice systems 8

J
Jones, Michael 25

K
Kang, Shimi 18, 19
Kava, social use of 45

L
learning in the home 18
  resources for 18
loan sharks 16, 22
Local Government Act 1974 40
Lotofale'ia Mangere Tongan Methodist Church 12

M
Manukia, Goll Fan 12, 13, 15
Manurewa Methodist Parish 13
Methodist Church of New Zealand 5, 32, 33
  Conference of as a law court 33
  laws and regulations of 7
Misinale, annual tithing 5, 13, 16

N
New Zealand Bill of Rights Act 29
Ngahe, Vaitu'ulala 13, 37

P
palangi church members 29
parents and children, open communication between 19
participation and democracy 43
Pasifika faith lore, recognition by legal system 35
Physical Welfare and Recreation Act 1937 40
Pole, Siosifa 37

R
religious beliefs 29

S
Sapate Ako, education week 46
sarcasm, use of by Pasifika people 49
Sharia law 8
social issues, Pasifika people to make own rules about 7
social legislation
  Pasifika concerns about 26, 27
social media platforms, use of by youth 19

T
Tamoaieta, Michael 48
theological questions, churches to decide for themselves 33
Tokoni'i, Tongan tradition of 11
Tonga 5
Treaty of Waitangi 32
Tuivasa-Sheck, Johnny 48

U
Uhila, 'Alipate 37
Umaga, Tana 14, 22

www.ingramcontent.com/pod-product-compliance
Lightning Source LLC
Chambersburg PA
CBHW071408070526
44578CB00002B/524